ONE PAGE
COMMUNICATOR

ONE PAGE COMMUNICATOR

Authored By,

Vasudevan Kidambi

Disclaimer

This book has been published with all reasonable efforts taken to make the material error-free after the consent of the author. This book is sold subject to the condition that it shall not, by way of trade or otherwise, be lent, resold, or otherwise circulated without the copyright owner's prior written consent in any form of binding or cover other than that in which it is published and without a similar condition including this condition being imposed on the subsequent purchaser and without limiting the rights under copyright reserved above, no part of this publication maybe reproduced, stored in or introduced into a retrieval system or transmitted in any form or by any other means without the ☐ permission of the copyright owner.

Registered Office- 907-Sneh Nagar, Sapna Sangeeta Road, Agrasen Square, Indore – 452001 (M.P.), India

Website: http://www.wingspublication.com

Email: mybook@wingspublication.com

First Published by WINGS PUBLICATION 2023

Copyright © Vasudevan Kidambi

Title : One Page Communicator

Price : AED 85 I INR 699 I $ 25

All Rights Reserved.

ISBN 978-81-19223-27-5

LIMITS OF LIABILITY/DISCLAIMER OF WARRANTY

Copyright © 2023 Vasudevan Kidambi

First Edition: 2023

Disclaimer

Although the publisher and the author have made every effort to ensure that the information in this book was correct at press time and while this publication is designed to provide accurate information in regard to the subject matter covered, the publisher and the author assume no responsibility for errors, inaccuracies, omissions, or any other inconsistencies herein and hereby disclaim any liability to any party for any loss, damage, or disruption caused by errors or omissions, whether such errors or omissions result from negligence, accident, or any other cause.

This publication is meant as a source of valuable information for the reader, however it is not meant as a substitute for direct expert assistance. If such level of assistance is required, the services of a competent professional should be sought.

Dedicated To

All my teachers & friends who constantly helped
in my continuous learning process and still
continue to find a way to give me more.

Review Request

Thank you for buying and reading my book!
If you enjoyed this book or found it useful,
I would be very grateful if you would post a short review
online and also share it on your social media platforms.

About the Author

 **Vasudevan Kidambi** is a highly inquisitive and analytical-minded professional renowned for his human-centric approach in solving problems. Widely recognized in business circles as the LAST-MILE MAN, he consistently delivers precise and effective solutions to his clients. With a genuine passion for storytelling, he leverages the power of compelling narratives to drive impactful change. One-page communication, a storytelling technique he ardently advocates, has proven to be instrumental in successful corporate communications.

Possessing exceptional connective skills and active listening capabilities, Vasudevan offers his expertise to top-tier organizations and executives, enabling them to achieve their objectives. His extensive experience in multinational corporations and consultancy work spans diverse areas of corporate operations. By combining this wealth of experience with his profound knowledge and insight into digital information, he facilitates business transformation by rebooting, realigning, and recovering.

Vasudevan excels in problem-solving through innovative methods, performing investigative data analysis, applying design thinking principles, and demonstrating an unwavering passion for data storytelling. He actively helps corporations foster a storytelling culture within their organizations. His comprehensive range of services includes business consulting, change management, content strategy, content marketing, and growth marketing. As the Managing Director of Navo Informatica Pvt. Ltd and Navo Management Consultants, he leads with collective wisdom and a structured, thoughtful approach, preparing organizations for the future.

With over three decades of invaluable corporate experience, Vasudevan has aided numerous regional and international companies in their digital and content transformation journeys. From adapting to the new normal and acquiring future-ready skills to implementing digital workflow automation and cognitive bots, his expertise continues to shape the success of countless enterprises.

You can find more about him @
https://www.linkedin.com/in/kidambivasudevan/

Table of Contents

Foreword

They say that parachutes and minds operate best when they are open. And this statement struck me in all my conversations with Vasudevan over the last eight years since I have known him.

I have known Vasu, as I call him, since my time as the Chief Customer & Community Officer at Emaar Properties PJSC. He was a consultant who delivered exciting solutions to my challenges.

Over the course of the next few years, I formed a great symbiotic relationship with him and asked him to collaborate with me on several large projects that I undertook at my own consulting firm. I knew that Vasu was the one person with whom I would enjoy working and consistently deliver what is in the best interests of the customer.

Several years later, the first part of my foreword still holds true. Even now, when I observe him interacting with some of our prestigious clients, I notice that he is an excellent listener absorbing the pain points and challenges of the customer and then delivering a simple, people-centric solution that not only alleviates the customers of their pain points but also leaves them immensely satisfied.

Among many of his passions, one is data. His talent is decoding and presenting complex data, numbers, and statistics in an easy-to-understand and consumed manner. It is no wonder he is often called the 'DOCTOR DATA' amongst business circles.

I have come to admire many aspects of Vasu; among these are his possession of an inquisitive and analytical mind, and his ability to listen purposefully and break down problems whilst being a genuine people's person at the same time are truly commendable.

I am sure this book will help understand the beauty of Data Storytelling, and you get to hear from the Master Data Storyteller himself.

Jeevan D'Mello, GDArch, CMCA, AMS, LSM, PCAM, D. Litt.

President, Global Leaders Today

CEO, Zenesis Corporation

Board Member, Rotary Club of Dubai

Board Member, Community Associations Institute, USA

Professor of Real Estate, Azetca University, Mexico

Executive Fellow, Woxsen University, India

About the Book

Interaction with other human beings forms the very foundation of society, and throughout the course of history, communication has been pivotal to our evolution. Among the various facets of human behavior that have undergone significant changes during this evolution, one aspect that stands out is communication itself.

In the realm of business, the key to transforming your dreams into success lies in effective communication. The ability to communicate effectively is an esteemed skill, particularly at middle management and senior executive levels.

This book centers around the paramount importance of effective communication within organizations, specifically focusing on the concept of 'One Page Communication' (OPC) and its core components: the audience, message, and purpose. Given the abundance of information across numerous channels and mediums, professionals must strive to deliver compelling communication that not only fits within a single page but also serves its intended purpose.

Through this book, my objective is to share my experience in creating concise and coherent communication for diverse scenarios across various industry verticals, thereby demonstrating their effectiveness in fulfilling their intended objectives.

Nine Things This Book Will Help You

1. Understanding the Importance of Organizing Thoughts for Effective Communication

   Recognizing the significance of organizing your thoughts before crafting your message.

2. Enhancing Clarity in Your Thought Process

   Developing a clear thought process to deliver impactful communication.

3. Appreciating Audience Awareness and Message Purpose

   Valuing the understanding of your audience and aligning your message with its purpose, while providing actionable content.

4. Mastering the Art of Narration and Storytelling

   Becoming skilled in the art of narration and storytelling to captivate your audience.

5. Eliminating Redundancy and Repetition in Communication

   Avoiding unnecessary redundancy and repetition in your communication.

6. Harnessing the Power of Visualization

   Recognizing the influence of visual elements such as colors, fonts, and images on message effectiveness, and learning how to utilize them effectively.

7. Embracing a Human-Centric Approach to Communication

   Prioritizing a human-centric approach to enhance your communication skills.

8.   Understanding the Benefits of Skill Practice and Habit Formation

Realizing the advantages of regular practice in transforming a skill into a habit.

9.   Becoming a Purposeful One Page Communicator

Transitioning into a purposeful communicator who can effectively convey their message within a concise one-page format.

> **"**
>
> *Good writing does not succeed or fall on the strength of its ability to persuade. It succeeds or fails on the strength of its ability to engage you, to make you think, to give you a glimpse into someone else's head*
>
> **Malcolm Gladwell**

1
CHALLENGES WITH WRITTEN COMMUNICATION AT THE WORKPLACE

In August 2020, Swedish job search engine Jobbland.se analysed more than 6.5 million jobs posted on LinkedIn. The analysis found that effective communication was cited in more than 2.3 million job openings. This figure far exceeds the next most-sought-after soft skill, the leadership, which was included in just over 1 million job postings. In fact, effective communication was cited in job postings at more than 35 times the frequency of other soft skills such as empathy, conflict resolution, adaptability, and dependability.

Delivering clarity in communication is one of the key competencies for organizational performance and yet remains one of the most critical challenges too. Every one of us thinks that we are good communicators. However, consciously, we all aspire to become better communicators.

You may have often encountered situations where your idea or proposal was either rejected or did not get the desired response. During my initial days with Samsung Middle East, I used to wonder and get frustrated as the huge efforts of creating presentation decks or proposals would not get the desired response. I would ask myself – "Why is my senior management unable to understand my proposal, the deep benefits for the brand, and the associated business advantages". Quickly enough I could decipher that it was not due to the proposal or the idea but owing to the ineffective communication of it.

Ineffective communication not only fails in its pursuits but also costs a lot of money to the organization. This is a huge unseen cost which cannot be fathomed by conventional methods. Also, the organizational leadership fails to see how ineffective communications hinder growth or result in missed opportunities.

David Grossman reported in "The Cost of Poor Communications" that a survey of 400 companies with 100,000 employees each cited an average loss per company of $62.4 million per year because of inadequate communication to and between employees.

Debra Hamilton asserted, in her article "Top Ten Email Blunders that Cost Companies Money," that miscommunication cost even smaller companies of 100 employees an average of $420,000 per year.

The questions that beg asking are:

1. *Is a poor form of communication common to most organizations?*

2. *Is there a strong needto improve effective communication skills?*

Generally, yes, and this is because there is no system to improve communication levels. The focus of most professionals is to create PowerPoint templates and slides, not on the 'improved thinking' that is instrumental in creating the right messaging. PowerPoint is only a tool to translate your thinking into written communication!

You should count yourself amongst the lucky ones if you are not constantly poked by your senior management asking to present your information on one single page. It becomes a daunting task if we don't understand the purpose behind such demands from the senior management.

So, what are some of the key challenges organizations face when it comes to written communication?

Lack of Clarity:

Many professionals tend to write lengthy content in an attempt to appear professional. However, this approach often hinders effective communication. Lengthy paragraphs and sentences require significant effort from the audience to comprehend the message. It is important to focus on articulating content clearly rather than adding unnecessary length.

Lack of Audience Awareness:

A common mistake is writing without considering the intended audience. Instead of making communication easy for the readers, we often prioritize showcasing ourselves.

Understanding the audience and tailoring the message accordingly is crucial for effective communication.

Redundancy in Communication:

Repeating information unnecessarily, similar to how we speak, can hinder effective communication. This error can be avoided by practicing precision and ensuring that the message is concise and to the point.

Lack of Purpose:

The purpose of communication is often overlooked due to a lack of awareness. Whether the goal is to inform or drive action, understanding the purpose and crafting the right messaging is essential. As professor Michael Pratt emphasizes, if people don't understand what you do, they devalue it.

Human-Centric, Actionable Communication:

Effective communication should always prioritize being human-centric, purpose-driven, easy to comprehend, presentable, comprehensive, complete, and most importantly, actionable. By incorporating these qualities into our communication, we can enhance its impact.

While we are on this subject, I have always followed the 6C's of communication and have found it to be extremely helpful in crafting compelling business communication.

The 6 Cs are:

1. ***Courtesy*** – This is about showing concern for the audience. Not just in emails, but in overall communication. This ensures goodwill. Goodwill comes with a feeling of confidence based on honesty and reliable service.

2. ***Clarity*** - means writing easy-to-read and easy-to-understand messages. Although I have elaborated on this in the previous pages, nothing makes communication as effective as the clarity of the message itself!

3. ***Conciseness*** – Make your communication as crisp and simple as possible. This may mean that you will have to do multiple iterations. Trust me, the effort is worth the result!

4. ***Concreteness*** – Convey what you want to and to whom you have to, concretely. This means that you MUST have a good understanding of your audience! This is the first step in piecing your communication together. Get this correct and the others are relatively easier.

5. ***Correctness*** – Accuracy! Remember, you are communicating either to share information or to drive action.

6. ***Completeness*** – Is your message complete? Does it carry all the necessary details/information that you wanted to share with your audience?

I have always found Kipling's Questions method as a standard framework to qualify the completeness of my communication. I will detail this method in the coming chapters.

Summary:

1. Communication is a challenge even today in many organizations

2. Improving this skill not only ensures effectiveness in the organization but also saves hundreds of hours for the organization

3. A concise form of communication within the confines of 'One Page' is possible and efficient too, the skill this book aims to impart.

"

To effectively communicate, we must realize that we are all different in the way we perceive the world and use this understanding as a guide to our communication with others

Tony Robbins

2

THE 3 KEY ELEMENTS OF EFFECTIVE COMMUNICATION

In the post-pandemic new order, the traditional lines of communication have been disrupted. The world has witnessed a sharp surge in the appetite for enhancing communication skills. According to LinkedIn, the number of hours that users dedicate to learning communication-related courses has increased three-fold. Out of the platform's 16,400 online courses, 4 out of the top 20 most popular courses deal directly with communications skills.

As human interactions get more and more complex, the need for effective and enhanced levels of communication becomes crucial.

Here's a funny, yet interesting written conversation.

The first thing I did when I heard our great-granddaughter was born was to text my son: "You are a grand uncle!"

He texted me back immediately: "Thank you. What did I do?"

Peggy Klasse

Imagine if this is the communication chaos within a family, how it could be within an organization, especially if you are writing to diverse people, you may not even know!

Hence, the **golden rule** for any form of communication – oral or written- is to have a clear understanding of three elements:

1.   **Audience (Who)**

2.   **Message (What)**

3.   **Purpose of the communication (Why)**

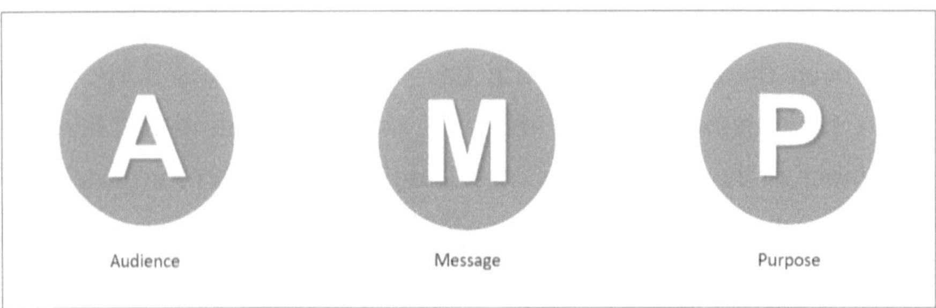

Figure 1.1 : The three key elements of effective communication

In the case of verbal communication, you have the audience in front of you and you can manoeuvre your communication depending on how the audience is responding to you. The lighting, setting, environment, tone, etc, can be adjusted and modified to improve communication effectiveness. (Except when you are in front of a camera that is recording your communique and where you have limited control over the environment or the audience. e.g., Zoom calls).

Often miscommunication is the result of a lack of clarity or flawed intent in the message that one attempts to communicate. In addition, if the articulation is poor, it does not result in what it has expected to achieve – the very purpose.

Effective communication is a two-way information-sharing process where one person sends a message that's easy for the receiver to understand. In business, effective communication helps individuals work more productively and efficiently.

The primary objective of effective communication is to promote comprehension and limit miscommunication and misinterpretation.

This is key to improving organizational performance and efficiency.

Effective Written Medium

For professional communication, written communication can take on many forms including email, text messages, memos, or letters.

They need to be more precise and explicit, and they also need to be effective to develop and enhance an organization's image and reputation.

Here are a few factors that you should be aware of when using the *written medium to make a strong connection with your audience.*

Prepare Powerful Sentences: Use an active voice, especially when seeking specific actions from the audience based on your communication.

Develop Logical Paragraphs: Construct well-crafted sentences and organize them into sections that explain different aspects of the topic.

Logically Connect Ideas: Maintain coherence and understanding by ensuring consistency in your thoughts. Avoid introducing new concepts abruptly, which could confuse the audience.

Revise and Proofread: After gathering your ideas, revise and restructure your communication to ensure a smooth flow, logical sequence, consistent tone, and overall clarity.

In essence, your written communication should be checked for Courtesy, Clarity, Conciseness, Concreteness, Correctness, Completeness!

I will elaborate on this and a few more characteristics of powerful writing in the subsequent chapter.

Summary:

1. The three key elements of communication are the Audience, Message, and Purpose.

2. Clarity on these elements greatly enhances the effectiveness of communication and helps achieve intended objectives.

3. Powerful sentences, logical paragraphs, connected ideas, and thorough revision and proofreading are crucial for impactful written communication.

"

Communication is only effective when we communicate in a way that is meaningful to the recipient, not ourselves

Rich Simmonds

3

KNOW YOUR AUDIENCE

L et me start this chapter by asking a question.

When you communicate, what is the purpose behind it?

1 -To do what you want to do

Or

2 - Want your audience to do something as a result of reading what you wrote.

I'm assuming that your answer is B) because it is the correct answer. And it involves the audience. In order to communicate effectively and to achieve your end objective, you must adapt to your audience. Thus, the importance of this chapter: **KNOW YOUR AUDIENCE.**

And this is where I want to bring in the relevance of being a **ONE-PAGE COMMUNICATOR!**

As we move into a more content/data-driven business world, audiences are seeking brevity in communication. Also, the fact that the world and its people have less patience and attention span to reading, one must develop the skills of being a One Page Communicator which we will learn in the later chapters of the book.

Not everyone in the audience is the same!

Audiences vary. They can be a small group, like a board, or a large group like an entire department or the organization itself. They can be reasonably homogeneous in what they already know or in what they are interested in, or they can be heterogeneous.

In some cases, you may know the audience very well or at least reasonably well, in some cases, you may not know them at all.

Knowing your audience gives you a clear insight of the language, visuals and other elements you can use to make your communication reach

Based on the above characteristics of the audience, here are a few other reasons why written communication is a skill that needs to be sharpened especially in the context of connecting with the audience.

1 - **We are enamoured by jargons!**

Over-complicated, unfamiliar and/or technical terms used daily while creating a false feeling that everyone uses our "language". Your audience can decode messages only within the context of their fields of experience. When the overlap is only a little, communication becomes difficult.

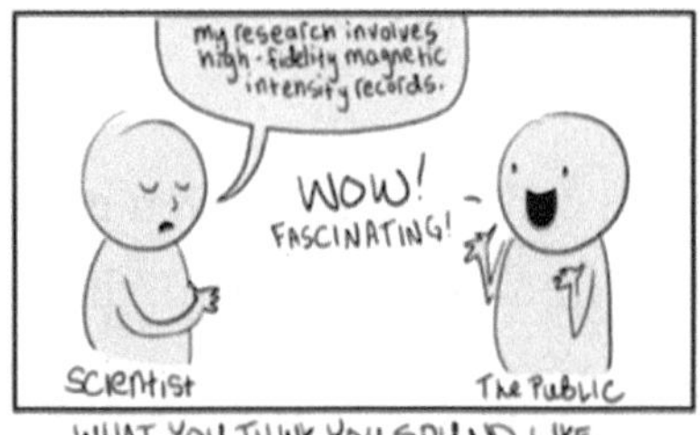

WHAT YOU THINK YOU SOUND LIKE.

WHAT YOU ACTUALLY SOUND LIKE.

2 - Physical barriers to non-verbal communication

Not having the ability to determine the non-verbal cues, gestures, posture, and general visual communication can make your communication less effective.

3 - Cultural differences

Although this may seem trivial at first, you just consider that you may be communicating with a range of people from different cultures. The messaging may be construed differently if you have not paid attention to this.

Figure 1.2: If you need something done, use the language of the audience!

While oral / spoken communication is supported by facial expressions and gestures, written communication is deprived of it all. That way, effectiveness in written communication is far harder. Also, in the case of the latter, enough attention has to be given to make communication as easy as possible and as simple as possible. Try and make it 'easy for the lazy'.

How do you identify with your audience and for what benefit?

1. Show empathy - Gain their Trust – At the risk of sounding cliched, by walking in their shoes, you identify with them. In today's fast-paced world, you must attempt to buy your audience's trust right from the word go and one great lever that can be used is empathy.

2. Resonate with them – to create Compelling messages – By identifying with your audience and being empathetic towards them allows you to think in the same way as them. This is the key to writing compelling messages.

3. Craft inspiring messages - Making them Act – The final benefit would be to make them act and so craft your message in a manner that will inspire requisite action from your audience. After all, the very purpose of communication is to either inform or get people to take an action

Let me tell you that not researching or identifying with your audience may result in catastrophe sometimes and may cost you dearly. In order to reach them or make them listen, understanding your audience is a skill that you must acquire.

Another important way of respecting the audience is providing an opportunity for your audience to react to your message and seek clarity when needed. If it is face-to-face communication, ask for feedback and ask questions to confirm that they comprehended the message.

If communicating in writing, provide a contact or resource to which they can turn for further information, as required.

Summary:

1. If your message is just for information or expecting an action, knowing your audience is very important.

2. Not only knowing but also identifying with them will help you to gain their trust, especially when you want them to act on your communication.

3. Jargons, cultural differences, and various barriers prevent us from connecting with people which we must be aware of while creating the message.

> ""
>
> *The first purpose of any business is the quality.*
> *Profit will come by itself*
>
> **Anonymous**

4

PURPOSE IS KEY

This brings us to the second element of effective communication: PURPOSE.

Powerful Communication Between People Plays A Critical Role In A Company's Bottom Line. Without It You're Toast! – Miti Ampoma

Every communication has an inherent purpose. The very reason of your written communication must be to catch the attention of your audience and convey your message with utmost clarity. To achieve this end, you, as the author of the communication, must have the control of the audience while the content is consumed. This is a bit technical, but doable.

In essence, the communication **'Message'** becomes ineffective when it ignores the clarity on **'Audience'** and **'Purpose'**.

Communicating with a purpose makes you focused on the message you want to relay and how well it is received. It becomes an open, honest form of communication that includes empathy as well.

Purposeful communication has a job to do. It applies to any form of communication, not only with team members. Every relationship you have as you run your business will be impacted by how your ideas come across. If your communication is purposeful then your message will deliver the objectives you want. You will be both heard and understood.

Professional communication may have many purposes. Some common professional communication purposes include informing, which includes providing good and bad news; instructing; requesting; and persuading.

While some communications have a single purpose, others may combine purposes or have a primary and a secondary purpose.

Purpose, along with other communication variables, helps you as a communicator to determine content.

Here are a few purposes of communication:

1. **Informing:** This is the primary purpose of most organizational communication. The focus should be on delivering the message in a concise and easily understandable manner, allowing anyone in the audience to grasp the information effortlessly.

2. **Inspiring Action:** This can be done in three ways:

    a. **Instructing:** Communication aimed at providing instructions requires ensuring the audience's complete understanding to facilitate appropriate application of concepts or procedures. (Further details in Chapter 6)

    b. **Persuading:** Leaders or individuals in leadership roles often communicate to persuade others, such as employees, partners, or board members.

    c. **Requesting:** When seeking information or specific actions from the audience, clear, concise, specific, and polite requests are crucial to achieve the desired outcomes.

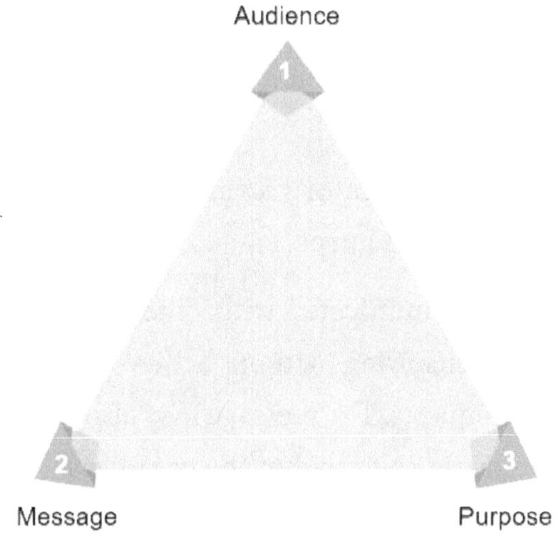

Figure 1.3: The holy triad of mastering your written communication!

As per R.E. Quinn, professionals communicate for four purposes[2]

- **Informing** - Static and Transactional – Task-Oriented

- **Directing** - Dynamic and Transactional – Task-oriented

- **Consulting** - Dynamic and Transformational – People-Oriented

- **Valuing** - Static and Transformational – People-Oriented

Content is linked inextricably with purpose and audience; purpose and audience determine content. The content/message of your communication may consist of anything viz., facts, statistics, anecdotes, testimonials, observations, examples, etc. Whatever the content, the message must be appropriate and interesting for the audience and purpose.

Summary:

1. Purpose is the core aspect of communication and demands careful consideration.

2. An impactful communicator recognizes the interplay between the audience, message, and purpose.

3. Professionals communicate with the purpose of providing information or inspiring action, achieved through instruction, persuasion, or requests. The message may also aim to direct, consult, or value individuals' roles within the organization.

4. Before sending out a message, determine the desired outcome you wish to achieve through your communication.

> **"**
>
> The fact that I'm using words doesn't necessarily mean that I'm saying anything.

Craig D. Lounsbrough

5

NARRATIVE DRIVEN MESSAGING

Again, before discussing this chapter, I would want to ask a few questions.

- *When you think about the best smartphone which brand comes to your mind? Either the iPhone or Samsung, right?*

- *When you think of the best sports accessories which brand comes to your mind? Is either Nike or Under Armour?*

- *When do you think of the best soft drink? Is it either Coca-Cola or Pepsi?*

- *Have you ever thought about how these brands have etched their names in consumers' minds?*

Well, primarily because they have been creating narratives that emotionally sway people. Your communication must also influence, and be able to get people to sit up, take notice, and in the appropriate cases, act.

So, how do we build this narrative in communication?

The answer lies in wearing the hat of a storyteller while crafting your messages. Human brains are wired for stories as they engage them. They build trust among the audience.

How to tell a story around your message?

Think of a logical structure of written communication that can interest people.

Below is a model to build great stories

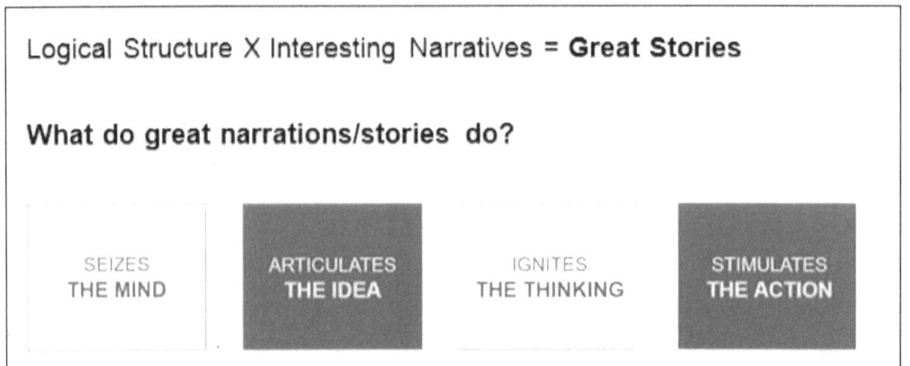

By communicating in an interesting form, every storyteller can, not only gain appreciation from their audience, but also make them get involved and act.

Whatever you want to share, engaging your audience matters. The data, numbers, and statistics are always part of the narrative, never the whole story. Great storytellers focus on connection, not just information.

Simply put, having a good narrative ensures your communication strikes a chord with your audience and delivers the message in a manner that it evokes interest and action from them.

Here is a quick guide on how to develop a story to specifically serve business needs.

Start with an end in mind (Have a problem, and a solution) – What was the setback? Who is the hero of your story and why? What were the driving vision and the proactive action? A good point of resolution will satisfy your audience and amplify your message.

Don't be afraid of emotions – Emotions are what make a story powerful. Use descriptive vocabulary so that your listeners can "see" what you are talking about. For example, rather than simply talking about "clients" describe the people involved, what were their challenges and personal benefits?

Keep it simple – Storytelling for business is different from writing a novel. You don't need plot twists. The most important thing is to keep it simple yet relatable. Talk about the problem and the solution, and how you can get the client there.

Make it relatable – As human beings, we engage more when we can relate. When telling your story, talk about how the challenge personally changed your way of thinking or shaped the outcome. Chances are your audience will be able to relate to the challenges, after all, every business experiences them. By making the story relatable, you are allowing your audience to make the story about them.

Here are a few elements that I apply when I create my narrative-based communication to ensure that my message is to *Seize the Mind, Articulate the Idea, Ignite the Thinking and Stimulate the Action![1]*

1. **Catch-Phrases:** Use catchphrases at the beginning of the communication to invoke your audience's curiosity. Dwell over what will keep your audience hooked to your communication till the end.

2. **Setting:** Every great story has a backdrop or a setting. Who, What, Where, When, What & Why? Be as descriptive as possible about these, to engage the audience.

3. **Spark:** That one critical event/situation that made you craft your message. This is the turning point that is making you communicate either to inform or to inspire action.

4. **Conclusion:** This section is all about what actions you want your audience to take. This is entirely dependent on the situation and the spark. Do remember to have clarity in your thinking when crafting this section!

Summary:

1. A narrative-driven message will seize the mind, articulate the idea, ignite the thinking, and stimulate the required action.

2. To create a good narrative, you need to don the cap of a storyteller as stories always engage the audience, build trust with them, involve them, make them listen, connect with them, and interest them to act.

3. A great story or business narrative, starts with a problem and finds a solution to it. Have emotions attached to it and it is simple and relatable.

4. A descriptive setting, some catchphrases, and a reason for the narrative with a good conclusion will provide you with the narrative you are looking for!

"

Effective Communication is 20% what you know and 80% how you feel about what you know.

Jim Rohn

TOOLKIT 1: UNDERSTANDING MECE

The MECE principle, pronounced by many as "ME-see", and pronounced by the author as "Meese" like Greece or niece, is a grouping principle for separating a set of items into subsets that are mutually exclusive and collectively exhaustive.

The MECE concept was developed in the late '60s by Barbara Minto at McKinsey & Company. Largely, the concept is being adopted by strategic consultants in segmentation & planning and several decision-making scenarios.

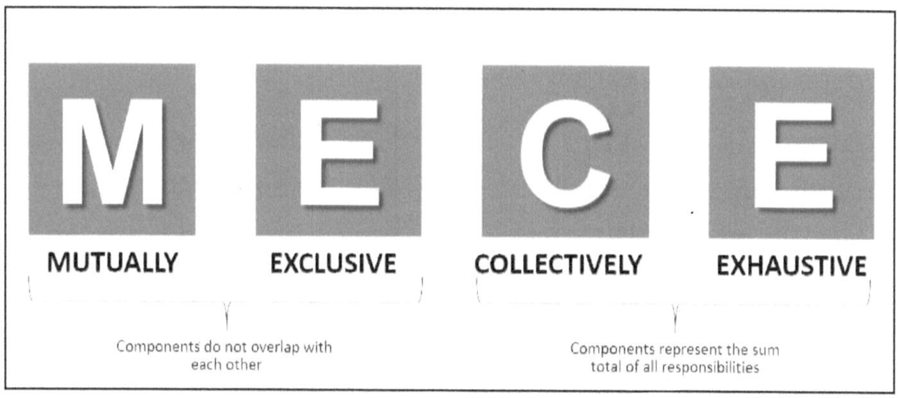

I fell in love with this ever since I came to know about it a decade ago and now applying MECE occurs to me very naturally. It structures the thought process, enables articulation, and enhances comprehension for the audience.

While thinking is an act common and natural to all, articulation involves techniques and MECE fits perfectly as a toolkit for one to follow.

There are four distinct advantages of applying MECE principle to communication and problem-solving:

1. Avoids duplication/redundancy to improve clarity

2. Ensures nothing is missed as the MECE application will confirm that all options are exhausted

3. Enables easy and quick understanding of the target audience

4. Facilitates brainstorming session

MECE comes very handy in evolving one-page communications and hence is considered as an important tool.

When designing a One Page Communication, one of the core intents is driving clarity. This can be achieved by ensuring the content is depicted without duplication/overlaps (mutually exclusive) and is complete in all respects (collectively exhaustive).

Although I speak of this as a very easy-to-use framework, it does take some amount of practice to start applying it. To repeat, this is more of a habit and a mindset that is achieved by doing it regularly. Only when you consciously apply this, to you will start seeing the results.

Let me share an illustration to show how things can be made simple by using the MECE even for a lengthy and verbose communication. And guess what, there cannot be a better One Page Communication as an output!

Illustration:

Task: How to transform a boring multi-page job description document (JD) into a usable tool, at the same time achieving all the purposes for which it is being created?

The underlying problem: By far, a Job Description document is a multi-page verbose document that is considered often 'boring to read'. Moreover, the long list of responsibilities in the document does not deliver the much-needed clarity and sections are not well grouped, in most cases. Different portions of a typical JD are used by different people at different times for different purposes – all these don't get articulated in a multi-page long-winded document.

Solution: One Page JD One Page Communicator: In designing a one-page JD, the entire content can be zoned with different colours ensuring that they are mutually exclusive and collectively exhaustive of all 'must have' details.

See Illustration 1 for a visual sample of a JD as a One Page Communication

Summary:

MECE – Mutually Exclusive and Collectively Exhaustive – is a technique that when applied improves the comprehension of the message by enhancing the articulation.

These principles have clear advantages when applied to communication and problem-solving:

1. Avoids duplication/redundancy

2. Ensures nothing is missed out as all options are exhausted

3. Quick and easy comprehension

4. Brainstorming is facilitated

Say a little and say it well

Irish Proverb

7 TOOLKIT 2 : KIPLING'S METHOD

Like I had indicated in the first chapter, a very important framework that I have been using over the years has been 'Kipling's Method' specifically for communication.

This is also known as the questioning method or the method of the Five Ws & 1H. 5W1H is an acronym in which every letter corresponds to a question: What, Who, Where, When, Why and How.

How to use it?

Rudyard Kipling used a set of questions to help trigger ideas and solve problems and immortalized them in the poem:

"I have six honest serving men, they taught me all I knew

I call them What and Where and When, And How and Why and Who"

The business world is more familiar with this as the 5W1H method.

As a communicator, you must try and answer all these questions:

a.   What are you communicating?

b.   Whom are you communicating with?

c.   Why are you communicating?

d.   How are you communicating?

e.   When are you communicating?

f.   Where are you communicating?

Do note: although the What, Who and Why are the critical ones,
you may not use the How, When and Where at all times
in the business scenarios.

This technique allows you to understand a situation, to discern a problem by analyzing all the aspects.

As outlined by Jean-Pierre Giraud on his blog, 'The big sales techniques",

"The 5W1H method allows you to discern the information needed to
better understand, encompass, clarify, structure,
frame a situation, as this way of thinking allows you to explore
all the dimensions from different perspectives". [1]

Therein lies the beauty of this toolkit. It allows you, as a communicator, to wrap your head around all the possible dimensions, when writing your message.

This also becomes a crucial part of the One Page Communication as it forces you to consider all aspects of the communication at a thought level.

Furthermore, this toolkit complements the MECE superbly, ensuring that your communication is not only complete but also exhaustive to your audience.

Summary:

1. Rudyard Kipling used 5W1H questions to get clarity on ideas and find solutions, the same can be used in solving business problems and or communicating them. However, we may use What, Who and Why mostly with others less often.

2. This method helps you to consider all the dimensions of the message you want to communicate and not leave any aspect while communicating concisely on a page.

"

Communication works for those who work at it

John Powell

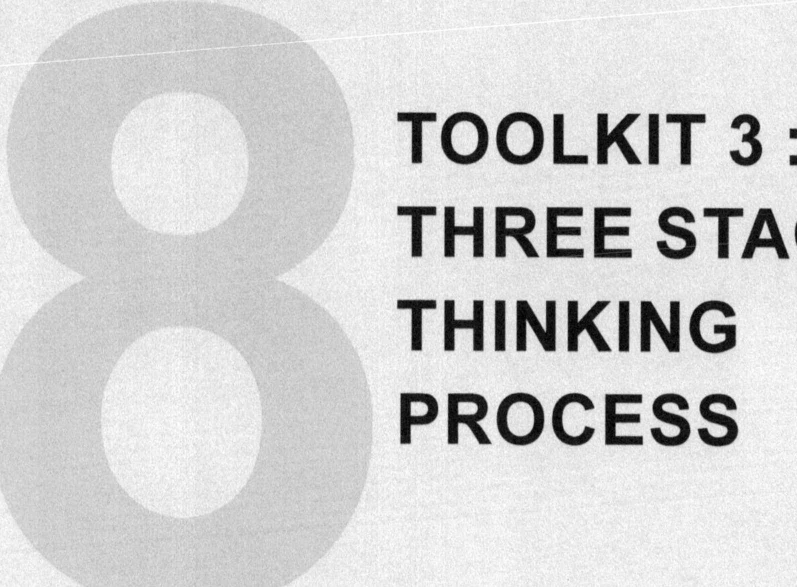

TOOLKIT 3 : THREE STAGE THINKING PROCESS

Earlier in this book, I opined that effective communication is not just about using PowerPoint or other documents to create your message, but it is more about how you apply your thinking to create that compelling message that you want to send across to your audience.

The question that pops up is, how can you develop this thinking?

Well, looks like it is not that difficult after all! Like everything in my experience of being an effective communicator, I realize it is about finding those processes and sticking with them.

There is a 3-stage process that I have developed to aid me in my thinking process when I embark on creating these One Page Communications, and they are:

1. **The Connect**

2. **The Narrative**

3. **The Visualization**

The Connect: Firstly, your communication is nothing but a story (remember the chapter on Narrative-based messaging?)

The true hallmark of a good storyteller is to find the links between the various characters and settings. All of your communication will have some characters/players/parts, and as an effective communicator always ensure that each one of them is connected to present an overall story.

The Narrative: This is a crucial piece and therefore, I have dedicated an entire chapter explaining the narrative in chapter 5.

The Visualization: This is the last of the 3-stage process where you will apply the artistice side artistic side of yours to ensure that your story/communication makes a telling impact on the audience.

A small heads-up: A lot of people I speak to say that they are far from being artistic. Well, I will share a few steps/ideas of how you can kindle the artist in you. And no, it is not that difficult.
If I can do it, anybody can do it!

My next endeavour is to explain what I do in each of these stages to help build my messaging/communication.

The Connect:

a. **Look for relationships** – Whether it is data or the characters in my message, I always use a drawing board technique to look at the relationship that exists. Now, I must admit, I was endowed with a curious mind, and I use that to full effect here. But I have come to realize that curiosity to know and connect can also be practiced. Start practicing!

b. **End in mind** – Any communication or messaging must have an end in mind. What is it that you want to achieve with this message? Unless you have this clarity in your mind, it will be difficult to put together a compelling message.

c. **Connect for the purpose** – Remember, 'Purpose' is key. What do you want your audience to do after consuming your communication? The different elements of your message must be connected at all times. Like a plan without a goal is just a wish, a communication without a purpose is just words without a soul.

The Narrative

As I have already explained in the previous chapter, your communication must be the one that,

SEIZE
THE MIND

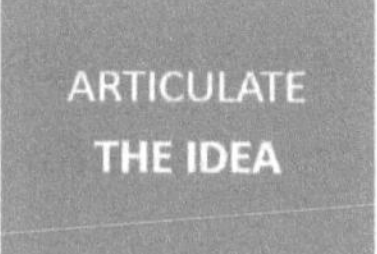

IGNITS
THE THINKING

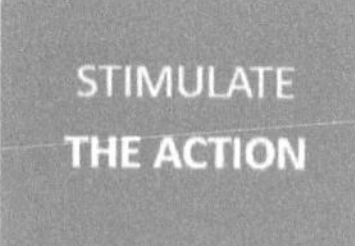

The Visualization

A -   **Colour choice** – This is key to set enforcing a visual thought in your audience. There is a science to colours, and it enables a telling impact on how your audience will react while reading your message. Especially in the case of creating a One-Page Communication, you should be able to use colours to help navigate the audience's minds to the desired section. With the rightful usage of colours, the comprehension of the content will be enhanced immensely.

I have explained this in the illustrations that are included at the end.

B -   **Infographic** – Symbolic communication is a form of communication that is deeply etched in the human brain as this was a very basic form of communication that we have had. Even as children growing up, we were able to understand concepts and ideas if we were taught in the form of symbols and shapes.

Infographics is an extension of this form of communication, and it makes it easy for the audience to connect and consume a message.

Do note, it is not simply the use of icons and pictures, it is about the use of suitable iconographs and its relevance to the message!

C - **Sequencing** – We as human beings, appreciate messages if they are logically sequenced since it will be easy to comprehend the message. Not only that, as a communicator, you can then direct the audience's mind to follow a set pattern, to evoke an emotion or action.

When you take care of these 3 stages while sculpting your messages, the outcome will be in the most effective format of communication.

Summary:

Key points to remember to direct the thinking process:

The 3 points thinking process: The Connect – The Narrative – The Visualization

1. The **Connect** happens, when there is established relationships between the points and the end results are kept in mind with the focus on the purpose of the communication.

2. The **Narrative** should be able to seize the mind, articulate the idea, ignite the mind and stimulate the requisite action where intended.

3. The **Visualization** will be enhanced by using proper colour choices and making use of infographics in the presentation and following a logical sequencing.

"

Even a super machine like an F1 car needs to be checked whether it is running fine!

Anonymous

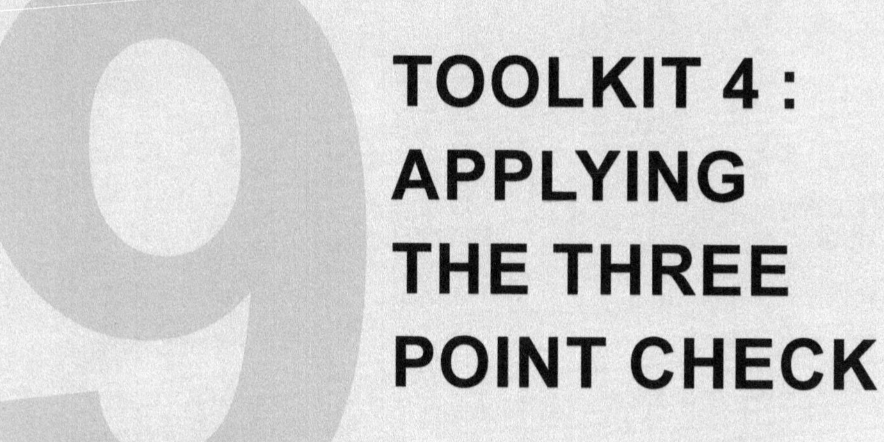

9

TOOLKIT 4 : APPLYING THE THREE POINT CHECK

One of the hallmarks of a good communicator is the ability to check the communication.

Often, writers employ or seek help from others to go over their writings to check if all is well. We, however, in the corporate, need to ensure a tight check mechanism for ourselves. Whilst I too struggled early on in this effort, I took inspiration from a story a few years ago.

The story:

Well, practice leads to perfection, which I too assure you based on my experience!

I practiced hard to develop a 3-point checklist to ensure if my messaging made complete and actionable sense.

The 3-point 'UPA' methodology is a combination of communication science and artful presentation that is aimed at weaving an appealing business story, to inspire action.

Understandable:

- Is your data story, empathetic to your audience? Will all sections of the audience be able to understand your message?

- Have you checked for the various factors that could affect understandability?

- Did your message qualify the AMP scanner?

If the answer to all the above questions is YES, then you have been successful in crafting a good message.

Presentable:

The next checkpoint is whether your story/message is presentable

- Does your story resonate with your audience emotionally?

- Have you looked at your story from the perspective of the audience?

- Did you qualify the Connect, Narrative, and Visualization stages of the thinking process, while you created the messaging/ communication?

If the answer to all the above questions is YES, you have created a presentable communication

Actionable:

- The only qualifier in this checkpoint is, does your story provide directions on what actions to take and when to take them?

There is a possibility that your message is only to inform and not to inspire action. So, be doubly sure of the messaging and the actions expected, thereafter.

MECE Influence:

To reiterate, this 3-point checklist too is inspired by the MECE approach – **Mutually Exclusive & Collectively Exhaustive.** You must now really be convinced of the MECE approach and how I have made it a part of my natural thought-process

Summary:

Practice leads to perfection. A three-point methodology I have practised to perfection is

1. **Understandable** – passed through AMP scanner

2. **Presentable** – Has all the requirements of Connect, Narrative, and Visualization to make it an appealing story for the intended audience

3. **Actionable** – If it is meant for inspiring action, should have clear instructions/directions.

When using this methodology to create your message, applying the MECE approach – Mutually Exclusive and Collectively Exhaustive - should be in your thoughts!

"

Seeing with the eyes of another, listening with the ears of another, and feeling with the heart of another

Alfred Adler

10

HUMAN CENTRIC
THINKING

Human-Centric Thinking is a concept that is very akin to Design Thinking. Design Thinking is based on a philosophy that empowers an individual or team to design products, services, systems, and experiences that address the core needs of those who experience a problem.

It is a concept that has been championed by Nobel Prize laureate Herbert Simon, developed, and taught by Stanford University to design effective and impactful solutions to challenges that are concentrated with a small group of people and those that are systemic.

What distinguishes Human-Centered Design from other problem-solving approaches is its obsessive focus on understanding the perspective of the person who experiences a problem, their needs, and whether the solution that has been designed for them is truly meeting their needs effectively or not.

There are 5 stages to Design Thinking

Well, something fantastic had to be a part of my skill set, so I went about trying to understand how I could use this to make communication simple yet, effective. Yes, this was one of the major inspirations for me to use the One Page Communicator as an effective organizational communication tool!

Here's how I developed the Human-Centered approach for creating compelling communication. The different stages of the process are:

1. **Empathize** – This stage is all about understanding people and trying to focus on a definable problem that this group of people have.

Empathy is crucial to a human-centred design process such as Story Telling. Empathy allows thinkers to set aside their own assumptions in order to gain insight into the audience and their needs, to trigger action

2. **Define** – At this stage, you will analyze your observations and synthesize them in order to define the core problems that you have identified

REMEMBER: Describe the problem statement in a HUMAN-CENTRED manner.

A well-defined problem statement is half the problem solved.

3. **Ideate** – You know your Audience & you have defined the problem. All of it is in a **HUMAN-CENTRIC way.** It is now time to have alternate views of the problem to come out with actionable(s).

4. **Prototype** – At this stage you will need to creatively find the connections between multiple smaller stories to create a grander, larger story. PROTOTYPING the first story is crucial to deliver the appropriate actionable insights to the audience.

5. **Test** – This is the **final stage**, and it is an **iterative process**, the actions/insights generated during the testing phase are often used to redefine one or more problems. This stage also gives a better understanding of the audience – how people think, behave, and feel – and to empathize!

Summary:

1. Design thinking or Human Centric thinking empowers an individual or team to design products, services, systems, and experiences by obsessively focusing on the individual or a group's perspective of a problem and finding a solution based on their needs and effectively solving it.

2. My human-centric approach to solving problems is by

- Empathising

- Designing

- Ideating

- Creating a Prototype and

- Testing

3. Application of this approach to create a one-page communication makes it a perfect communication tool.

> **"**
>
> *If you can say it in a paragraph, don't write a book*
>
> **Frank Sonnenberg**

11

THE POWER OF ONE PAGE COMMUNICATION

I am hugely inspired by the seminal book, 'Art of War' by Sun Tzu, the ancient Chinese military strategist. One sentence that I quote from his book is:

"If words of command are not clear and distinct; if orders are not thoroughly understood, the general is to blame"

So as a good communicator, it is imperative to ensure that your message is not only clear but also distinct.

Single page and comprehension benefit:

'Give it to me in a single page' is a very common ask by top management in the corporate world. In the early part of my career, I could not understand why they needed it that way. Only when I started communicating at a senior level did I understand that it increases and aids comprehension manifold.

One Page Communication is not about compressing bullet point texts of several sections into one page.

Sometimes, loading the entire page using every bit of the real estate space with content is, usually misunderstood as One Page Communication. **The objective of the One Page Communication is contrary!**

To make this One Page Communication powerful, there are a few elements that you must take care of:

Simplicity – This is such a revered virtue in communication, and I cannot stress it enough. The essence of communication is to ensure the audience understands your message. So, I always ***KISS! Keep It Short & Simple!***

Usability - As previously stated, the element of purpose of our communication demands its unnegotiable attention. The OPC should fulfil its objective – information or initiate action.

Clarity – To avoid misinterpretation, dissatisfaction, confusion and loss, ensuring clarity in your message is of utmost importance in every message you craft.

Structured Story Flow – Nothing beats a great story like a loose storyline/ flow. One Page Communication is a great tool to emphasize to yourself the need to make the story more structured.

Zoning – Each part of the One-Page must fulfil a certain objective, When the purpose of the communication is well defined, it enables quicker decision-making.

<u>**Additional pointers to keep in mind**</u>:

- It must be comprehensive not at the cost of visual simplicity.

- It must be clear without any redundancy or confusion.

What does the One Page Communication help you with?

The benefits are immense by way of achieving better communication of your message. However, the greatest benefit an organization gets is :

The audience get to see the specific parts that could apply only to them and at the same time, 'the whole' as well, ***all of this in a single glance.***

Summary:

1. Single-page communication benefits better comprehension and it is not just reducing the font size or cramming all information on one page.

2. Keeping the content simple, making a structured flow in the presentation, and zoning for each objective are the elements of a One Page Communication.

3. Able to see the whole as well as specific part at a single glance is the greatest benefit.

"

Magic is believing in yourself. If you can do that, you can make anything happen.

Johann Wolfgang Von Goethe

12

IT IS TIME TO DO THE MAGIC

I recently chanced upon a book, Atomic Habits by James Clear. A sentence in that book hit me like a train at full speed.

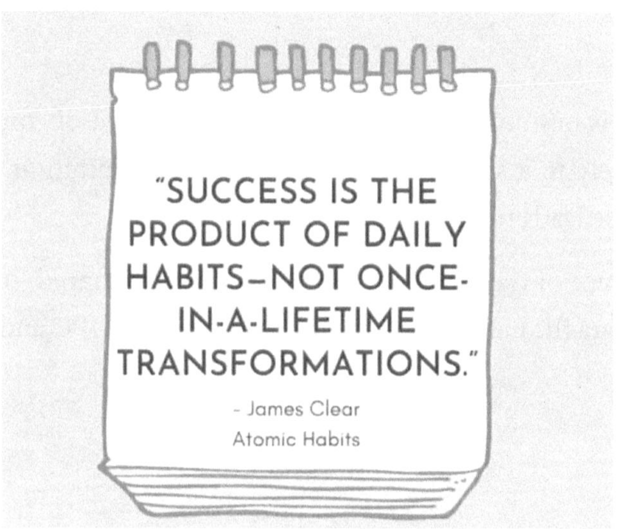

Why am I bringing this sentence here?

Well, I did not wake up one day and become the Master Storyteller that I am today. I too took inspiration from the experiences that I had with people, the books I read, and the videos I watched and then developed my skill.

At the very beginning, I had said that my endeavour through this book is to share my experiences and help you develop this fantastic skill of becoming an articulate One Page Communicator.

That being said, just by reading this book, you may be inspired to become a better communicator, but you will have to practice the process and respect it at all times, to develop this as a habit.

I have shared 4 toolkits and other ideas and frameworks in this book. Once you start putting them all into practice, **YOU WILL SEE THE MAGIC HAPPEN!**

Summary:

1. Rome is not built in a day. To get into the habit of communicating concisely in a single page, this book is an inspiration, and regular practice leads to perfection of the skill.

2. Make use of the toolkits and my experiences shared in the book to inculcate the habit of communicating through OPC and develop the skill.

"

Action is the foundational key to all success.

Picasso

13

YOU ARE NOW A ONE PAGE COMMUNICATOR

Well, here we are!

Over the last 12 chapters, I have walked you through the theory of how to become an effective One Page Communicator.

I have explained the importance of concise communication in professional life and how it benefits everyone involved. To improve the effectiveness of the communication we need to know the 'AMP'. Knowing your AMP – Audience, Message, and Purpose sharpens the content you want to communicate.

I have also elaborated on the need to have a good narrative and how storytelling ability enhances and drives the narrative. A good story will have a descriptive setting, some catchphrases, and a reason for the narrative with a good conclusion. The Narrative should be able to seize the mind, articulate the idea, ignite the mind and stimulate the requisite action.

Toolkits:

I have presented you with four toolkits to use while preparing your communication.

Applying MECE – 'Mutually Exclusive and Collectively Exhaustive' -technique along with Kipling's 5Ws and 1H method will make your communication not only whole but also exhaustive.

The 3-stage thinking process – The Connect, the Narrative and Visualization- will help you to create the best content for the consumption of your audience resulting in fulfilling the intended purpose.

The 3-point checking with UPA – the content is Understandable, Presentable and Actionable- will hit the bull's eye, if done correctly.

Having the human-centric (with empathy) and design thinking approach (Ideate, make a Prototype and Test) coupled with the idea of 'single window comprehension' is the road to the OPC destination, as you have understood by now.

From this chapter onwards, the focus will only be on helping you visualize how I put all these theories into practice.

I also want to share with you a few fine examples of how I have turned some extremely lengthy, verbose content into an effective One Page Communication.

Summary:

Through this book, you have received all the tips and tools to become a One Page Communicator. Now, look at the following illustrations which will show you how boring and lengthy content can be presented in a visually pleasing and concise manner for easy consumption/use.

I have also explained the challenges we faced in each situation and how using the OPC way of communication offered some advantages over the traditional way of presenting the information.

Illustrations

Illustration -1: OPC FOR JOB DESCRIPTION

Introduction

A Job Description document in any organization is a basic document detailing the scope, duties, roles & responsibilities, and working conditions relating to a particular job. It further details the skills and qualification-related details to qualify a person for the job.

While enormous efforts get underway to prepare a Job Description and place it through various approval processes, its usability has been always been low in most organizations.

In most middle and senior-level cadres in the organization, the Job Description runs into two and sometimes three pages.

A typical Job Description for a senior manager would look like the one shown below:

JOB DESCRIPTION
ASSISTANT PROPERTY MANAGER

Job Functions

The purpose of the Assistant Property Manager (APM) position is to assist with the day-to-day functions of the property management department and the functions of the Property Manager to which he/she is assigned. The focus of job is to support the Property Manager in all aspects of management pertaining to the client's property. The APM is the liaison between the tenants and the Property Manager for maintenance and many tenant issues at commercial and residential properties.

Job Responsibilities include, but are not limited to:
- Writing work orders for Maintenance department based on information from tenants, technicians or based on information gathered from site visits
- Drafting Memos and/or making phone calls to Tenants related to lease issues and preventative maintenance scheduling
- Issuing keys to technicians/vendors, keeping logs of who has keys and ensuring return of said keys
- Perform all necessary functions to facilitate Tenant "Move In" and "Move Out" procedures including:
  - Informing the tenant of the lease obligations and present them with keys, notifying them as their expiration date approaches & informing them of their obligations upon move out
  - Performing walk-outs of units and writing work orders related to turnovers
  - Processing Security deposit returns
- Maintain logs related to:
  - Essential Lead Maintenance (EMP)
  - Project Lists for individual properties
  - Unit Turnover List
- Obtaining Bids – Snow removal, landscaping, rubbish & maintenance/repairs
- Perform inspections and replenish inventory where necessary

Other duties include office support and on-call emergency response. Due to the location of our client properties and the requirement of emergency response, the candidate must live within 45 minutes driving distance of Neville's office.

This description is meant to be an outline and is not intended to list all duties and responsibilities.

Qualifications

The ideal candidate will be proficient in the Microsoft Office Suite with an emphasis on Excel, Word and Outlook. The candidate must have experience associated with administrative duties

The Challenge

The verbose Job Description document is less appealing to read. Further, a long list of roles & responsibilities is, at most times, difficult to comprehend.

While the document may be functionally meeting its requirement, it scores low on usability and hence finds itself not serving its intended purpose. This leads to the document not getting reviewed periodically leading to stale Job Description documents.

The author's thinking behind OPC creation

- Making the critical document more appealing and usable

- Zone the document based on purpose using a colour variation

- Make the document quick, easy, and effortless to use by different people at different times for different purposes

OPC Advantage

- Multiple objectives of the document got vividly clarified increasing the usability manifold

- Roles and responsibilities get far more well-defined, segmented, and prioritized delivering clarity to the position and the person holding the position

- Modification/review gets a lot more easier due to zoning and sectioning.

- All-in-one page drives faster comprehension

JOB TITLE: Assistant Property Manager   **DIVISION:** Urban Planning   **DEPARTMENT:** Property Management   REF. DOC_ 20222 GRADE 2   JD OPC

ROLES & RESPONSIBILITIES

MANAGERIAL

- **Writing** work orders for the Maintenance department based on information from tenants, technicians or based on information gathered from site visits
- **Drafting** memos and/or making phone calls to Tenants related to lease issues and preventive maintenance scheduling
- **Issuing** keys to technicians/vendors keeping logs of who has keys and ensuring the return of said keys
- **Perform** all necessary functions to facilitate Tenant "Move in" and "Move Out" procedures
- **Office support** and on-call emergency response
- **Performs** inspections and replenish inventory where necessary

FINANCIAL

- **Manage** Budgets by exercising due diligence and cost control to ensure expenses do not exceed the budget
- **Implement strategies** to maximize revenue
- **Advise** the management regularly of all processes by producing relevant reports about the department

OPERATIONAL

- **Implements** projects to ensure that the mandates are executed in an effective manner consistent with company's policies.
- **Regular inspections/audits** of the assigned building and drive proactive resolutions to ensure standards are always maintained.
- **Plans** monthly meetings with senior Management to drive overall site management
- **Supervise** the team members, to monitor their adherence to company policy and standards in achieving goals

KNOW YOUR JOB

PURPOSE OF THE JOB

Assist with day-to-day functions of the Property Management Department and the functions of the Property Manager to which he/she is assigned.
Focus is to support the Property Manager in all aspect of management pertaining to the client's property.

REPORTING STRUCTURE

Reports to: COO

Supervises: Properties Department

KEY INTERACTIONS

- CEO
- Customers
- Managers
- Department staff

SUCCESS FACTORS

KPI

- <Insert KPIs Here>

CHECKLIST

1. Gender:
2. Nationality:

PREFERENCES

IDEAL PERSONA

QUALIFICATIONS

- **Master's degree** or equivalent experience in a complimentary discipline
- **Proficient** in Microsoft Office Suite with an emphasis on Excel Word and Outlook

EXPERIENCE

- 15 years

SKILLS

- Excellent written and verbal communication
- Leadership and organizational skills
- Ability to work in a dynamic environment

CORE COMPETENCIES

- Understanding Business(Level 5 - Expert)
- People Champion (Level 4 - Expert)
- Effective Planning (Level 3 – Competent)
- Driving Excellence (Level 5 - Proficient)
- Managing Change (Level 5 – Expert)

Performance related information   Job Role, Functional Information   Hiring, JD related information

Illustration 2: OPC for EMERGENCY RESPONSE PLAN (CRISIS MANAGEMENT)

Introduction

Often when an emergency strikes, the speed of action, accuracy, and team efforts plays a crucial role in containing the damages significantly. To meet this, large organizations have formulated a well-structured 'Emergency Response Plan' document that clearly lays out who should do what at times when an emergency strikes.

Such a document is generally a verbose document and is kept physically (printout) or digitally stored. Also, to manage emergency response, several stakeholders get involved who will work in tandem without loss of precious time and act cohesively.

The situation calls for each one to know what they have to do and what someone else has to perform to ensure the dependency factor.

In its current form (verbose document running to few pages), the person acting at the time of emergency must find the document, and the relevant section, and read the instructions pertaining to oneself and the team. This takes time and every second is critical.

As such, the document in its form lacks 'usability' and fails to deliver the much-needed speed of comprehension.

A typical emergency response plan document could be like the one shown below:

Persons/agencies	Roles & Responsibilities
IM	• Takes control of the CCC&DCC, activates the Emergency Response Plan and have the crisis management team at the center. • Implement the ERP, and ensure continued compliance with the plan • Ensure the availability of adequate resources, staffing and backup staff, and arrange call-out of essential personnel • Direct the evacuation in consultation with the local IC and key personnel • Receive updates of personnel accountability and identification of missing individual(s) • Receive updates on control measures taken by the IC and monitor effectiveness • Assess the situation and direct actions to minimize damage and loss of life. • Maintain contact with upper management • Collect information necessary for government reporting and legal matters.
IC	• Ensure the safety and proper use of PPE by all responders • Develop and implement control tactics • Approve the use of all emergency-related resources • Keep the IM informed • Evaluate mutual aid needs and request assistance through the IM • Maintain headcount and identify missing individuals.
Security	• Determine the level of emergency & notify emergency response personnel (i.e. Civil Defense & Medical) • Dispatch security personnel & vehicles to diverge traffic and secure scene • Have radios available for communication.
Civil Defense	• Provide equipment (i.e. trucks, fire extinguishers, aerial ladders) • Sets up and carry out rescue and firefighting plan.
Medical Services	• Provide ambulances to treat and transfer casualties to nearest medical centers.
Property Management	• When necessary, arrange sheltering for tenants • Provide Logistical support, such as catering, or as requested by the IM
HSE	• Provide layouts to the Civil Defense • Provide the civil defense with plans and early measures taken.
Procurement	• Obtain additional emergency response supplies per the request of the of the IM.
Crisis Communication Management team*	• *Communication Crisis Management Team (CCMT) team meeting to be held immediately/Leadership taskforce team to be activated: CEO, HR, Internal Communications, External Communications, Health & Safety/Security Team.* • *Ensure Taskforce team has engaged with Local Emergency/Fire Services Conference call with relevant/involved managers/stakeholders to be convened.* • *Activate media and social media monitoring and prepare swift and factual responses to counter speculation.* • *Begin drafting an initial PROACTIVE 'holding statement'.* • *Email the holding statement to local/domestic media.*

The Challenge

An emergency strikes when it is least expected, and the stakeholders who need to respond to the situation need to have access to a plan of action. Although organizations will have a response plan (as it is mandatory), these are not very user-friendly and are written as verbose documents. In a crisis situation, the human mind is not very capable of consuming lengthy content to arrive at desired actions.

While the document may be functionally meeting its requirement, it scores low on usability and hence finds itself not serving its intended purpose. This leads to the document not getting reviewed periodically and becomes unusable.

The author's thinking behind OPC creation

- Most crucial in case of emergency is 'the actor' and 'the action'.

- Making the critical document more appealing and usable.

- Zone the document based on 'actor & action'.

- Help high-speed comprehension and action through OPC.

OPC Advantage

- Driving clarity through 'actor & action' approach.

- Every actor swiftly gets to know his/her action as well as that of the team members' actions for a concerted and rapid response.

- Modification/review gets a lot more easier due to zoning and sectioning.

- All-in-one page drives faster comprehension.

Crisis Management
Large Fire

CCC → Command Control Center   PPE → Personal Protective Equipment

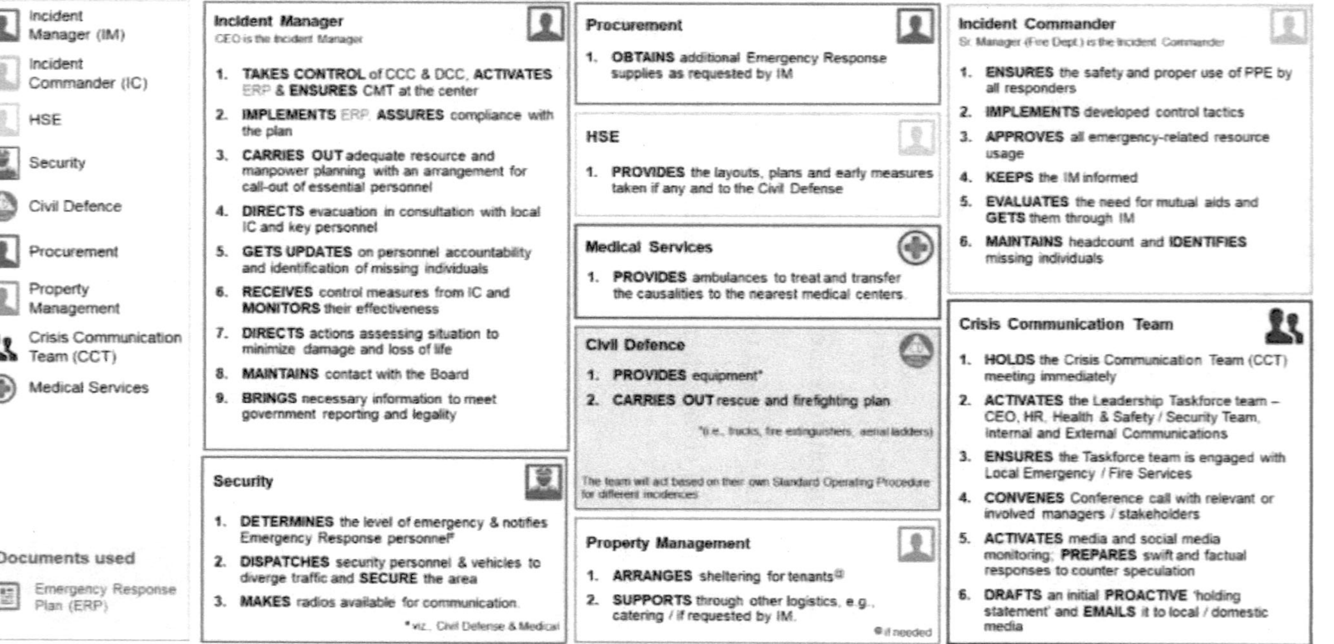

Incident Manager (IM)

Incident Commander (IC)

HSE

Security

Civil Defence

Procurement

Property Management

Crisis Communication Team (CCT)

Medical Services

Documents used

Emergency Response Plan (ERP)

Incident Manager
CEO is the Incident Manager

1. **TAKES CONTROL** of CCC & DCC, **ACTIVATES** ERP & **ENSURES** CMT at the center
2. **IMPLEMENTS** ERP. **ASSURES** compliance with the plan
3. **CARRIES OUT** adequate resource and manpower planning with an arrangement for call-out of essential personnel
4. **DIRECTS** evacuation in consultation with local IC and key personnel
5. **GETS UPDATES** on personnel accountability and identification of missing individuals
6. **RECEIVES** control measures from IC and **MONITORS** their effectiveness
7. **DIRECTS** actions assessing situation to minimize damage and loss of life
8. **MAINTAINS** contact with the Board
9. **BRINGS** necessary information to meet government reporting and legality

Security

1. **DETERMINES** the level of emergency & notifies Emergency Response personnel*
2. **DISPATCHES** security personnel & vehicles to diverge traffic and **SECURE** the area
3. **MAKES** radios available for communication.

*viz., Civil Defense & Medical

Procurement

1. **OBTAINS** additional Emergency Response supplies as requested by IM

HSE

1. **PROVIDES** the layouts, plans and early measures taken if any and to the Civil Defense

Medical Services

1. **PROVIDES** ambulances to treat and transfer the causalities to the nearest medical centers.

Civil Defence

1. **PROVIDES** equipment*
2. **CARRIES OUT** rescue and firefighting plan

*(i.e., trucks, fire extinguishers, aerial ladders)

The team will act based on their own Standard Operating Procedure for different incidences

Property Management

1. **ARRANGES** sheltering for tenants@
2. **SUPPORTS** through other logistics, e.g., catering / if requested by IM.

@ if needed

Incident Commander
Sr. Manager (Fire Dept.) is the Incident Commander

1. **ENSURES** the safety and proper use of PPE by all responders
2. **IMPLEMENTS** developed control tactics
3. **APPROVES** all emergency-related resource usage
4. **KEEPS** the IM informed
5. **EVALUATES** the need for mutual aids and **GETS** them through IM
6. **MAINTAINS** headcount and **IDENTIFIES** missing individuals

Crisis Communication Team

1. **HOLDS** the Crisis Communication Team (CCT) meeting immediately
2. **ACTIVATES** the Leadership Taskforce team – CEO, HR, Health & Safety / Security Team, internal and External Communications
3. **ENSURES** the Taskforce team is engaged with Local Emergency / Fire Services
4. **CONVENES** Conference call with relevant or involved managers / stakeholders
5. **ACTIVATES** media and social media monitoring; **PREPARES** swift and factual responses to counter speculation
6. **DRAFTS** an initial **PROACTIVE** 'holding statement' and **EMAILS** it to local / domestic media

Illustration 3: OPC FOR BUSINESS STORY

Introduction

I am sure some of you may have come across a situation where you would have access to a plethora of reports and insight documents. These reports will be generated by different departments or even external agencies. As a decision-maker, it poses a challenge of seeing all these reports at various points and connecting them to one another to arrive at a decision.

Beyond this, these various scenarios must be cascaded to the respective teams to enable them to take appropriate actions.

Essentially, the story must give clarity on the current situation

The Challenges -

1. Plethora of reports and each of them being conceived as a silo point

2. Ill-conceived storylines that fail to inspire the audience into action

3. A communication plan that packs ideas in a 'single window view'

4. The information existing across different pages and reports makes it complex to comprehend

The author's thinking behind OPC creation

The information from various sources such as market reports, trends data, RTM data, OGSM data, financial reports etc should be brought together into a single window view by applying all the principles of OPC.

The usage of colours, especially Red, Amber, and Green (RAG) is universal in its understanding to show the impact of various actions as per their importance and urgency.

Blending the different stories using a common thread to show the interlink and ensure that the audience see what the presenter wants them to focus on.

OPC Advantage

- Bringing disparate data points into a single window view

- Enabling clarity, simplicity, and usability of information in a crisp format

- Enabling a visual narrative to help the audience understand the impact of various actions

- A clear and fluid idea of where the organization can play and how it can win

BUSINESS REALITY OPC – SOAP CATEGORY

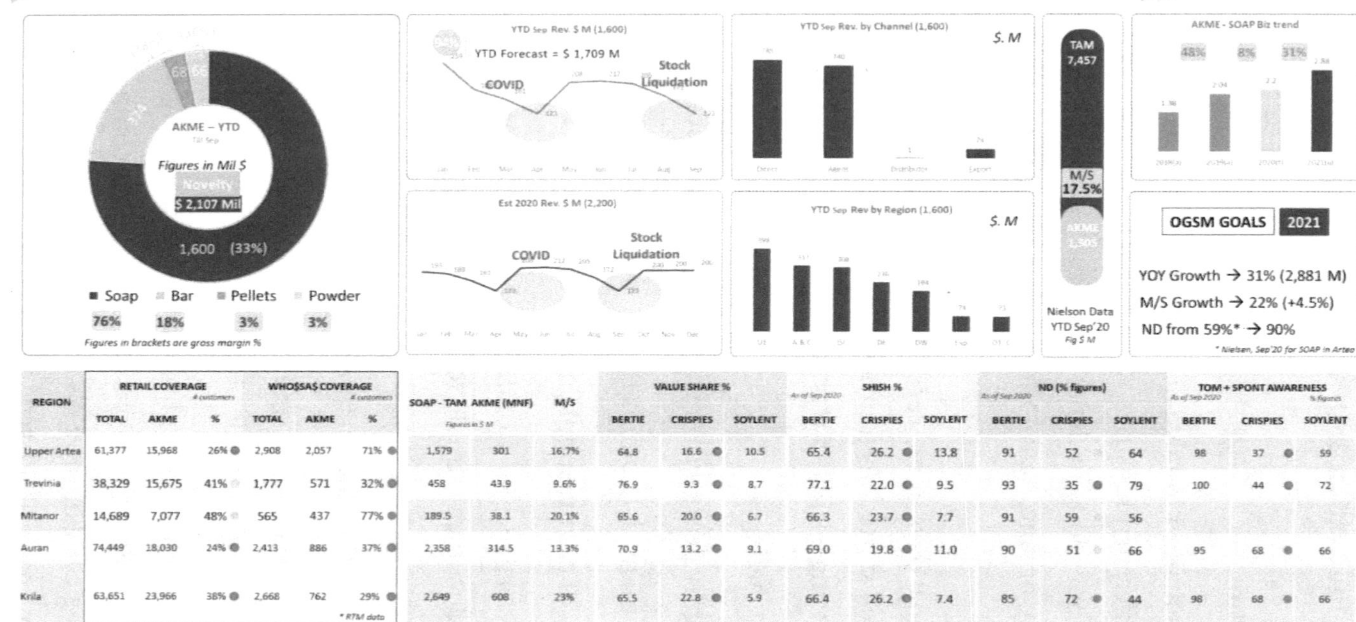

REGION	RETAIL COVERAGE (# customers)			WHOSA COVERAGE (# customers)			SOAP - TAM (Figures in $ M)	AKME (MNF)	M/S	VALUE SHARE % (As of Sep 2020)			SHISH % (As of Sep 2020)			ND (% figures) (As of Sep 2020)			TOM + SPONT AWARENESS (As of Sep 2020)		
	TOTAL	AKME	%	TOTAL	AKME	%				BERTIE	CRISPIES	SOYLENT	BERTIE	CRISPIES	SOYLENT	BERTIE	CRISPIES	SOYLENT	BERTIE	CRISPIES	SOYLENT
Upper Artea	61,377	15,968	26%	2,908	2,057	71%	1,579	301	16.7%	64.8	16.6	10.5	65.4	26.2	13.8	91	52	64	98	37	59
Trevinia	38,329	15,675	41%	1,777	571	32%	458	43.9	9.6%	76.9	9.3	8.7	77.1	22.0	9.5	93	35	79	100	44	72
Mitanor	14,689	7,077	48%	565	437	77%	189.5	38.1	20.1%	65.6	20.0	6.7	66.3	23.7	7.7	91	59	56			
Auran	74,449	18,030	24%	2,413	886	37%	2,358	314.5	13.3%	70.9	13.2	9.1	69.0	19.8	11.0	90	51	66	95	68	66
Krila	63,651	23,966	38%	2,668	762	29%	2,649	608	23%	65.5	22.8	5.9	66.4	26.2	7.4	85	72	44	98	68	66

* RTM data

Illustration 4: OPC FOR BUSINESS LANDSCAPE

Introduction

As a consultant, I indulge in many conversations with senior executives across different industries. One typical challenge most of them have stated is 'how do I condense a 40-page report into a crisp document to enable my organization to have a better understanding of the business landscape'.

In the initial days of my career, I too was plagued by this challenge. It is only when I started my journey as a consultant, that I developed this idea of condensing a lengthy report into a crisp one-page document.

The Challeges

- Lengthy decks with a whole lot of information

- Too many data points that do not have a correlation to each other

- Lack of clarity, simplicity, and usability

- Over-reliance on the intelligence of the audience, rather than making the document simple for consumption across a large spectrum of people

The author's thinking behind OPC creation

Making an exhaustive multipage research report into an easy-to-comprehend format is the objective.

The detailed thinking culminated at deciding that applying Kipling's method will be the best way to make this OPC a comprehensive document. The strategic use of the 5Ws and 1H enables the audience to understand the various parts of the report with ease.

OPC Advantage

- Easy correlation of the various elements of a report

- Driving clarity through a simple approach delivered in a 'single window view'

- Ease of understanding a complex landscape, especially if the territory is large

CATEGORY - NUTS - 5W & 1H OF CONSUMPTION

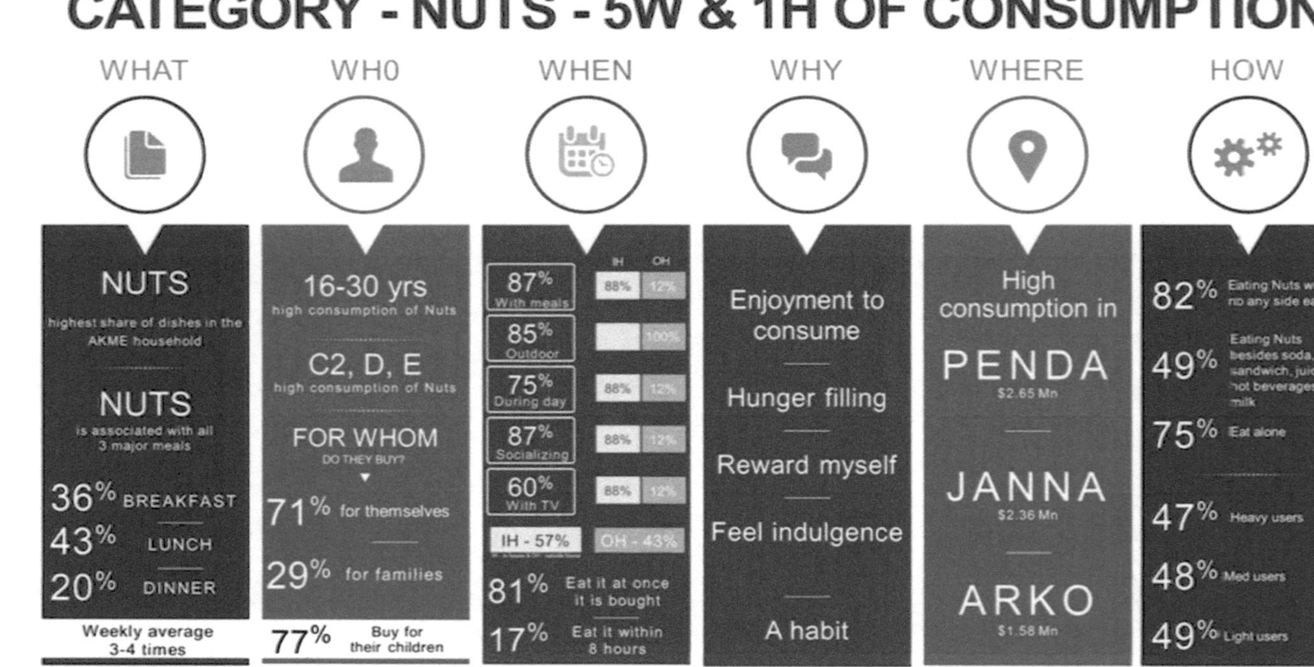

References

Chapter 1.0

https://www.shrm.org/resourcesandtools/hr-topics/behavioral-competencies/communication/pages/the-cost-of-poor-communications.aspx

Poor written communication and its crippling effects on business

https://www.costercontent.co.uk/blog/poor-written-communication

The High Cost of Poor Writing (About $400 Billion)

https://thinkgrowth.org/the-high-cost-of-poor-writing-about-400-billion-559e9fe5f735

The cost of poor communication

https://www.business2community.com/communications/the-cost-of-poor-communication-02420934

The true cost of poor communication

https://www.forbes.com/sites/forbescoachescouncil/2017/11/15/the-true-cost-of-poor-communication/?sh=59d826e920ab

Key Issues in Written Business Communication

https://smallbusiness.chron.com/key-issues-written-business-communication-21973.html

The Cost of Poor Communications

https://www.shrm.org/resourcesandtools/hr-topics/behavioral-competencies/communication/pages/the-cost-of-poor-communications.aspx

This is the most in demand skills on job listing right now

https://www.fastcompany.com/90556370/this-is-the-most-in-demand-skill-in-job-listings-right-now

Chapter 2.0

The skills companies are hiring for – Right now (LinkedIn Learning Blog)

https://www.linkedin.com/business/learning/blog/career-success-tips/skills-companies-are-hiring-for-right-now?src=afflilpar&veh=aff_src.affilpar_c.partners_pkw.10078_plc.Skimbit%20Ltd._pcrid.fastcompany.com_learning&trk=aff_src.afflilpar_c.partners_pkw.10078_plc.Skimbit%20Ltd._pcrid.fastcompany.com_learning&clickid=Rn4TJ91ZzxyLWo8wUx0Mo3EqUkGSgZwFA31%3AS40&mcid=6851962469594763264&irgwc=1

https://thebusinessprofessor.com/en_US/communications-negotiations/process-for-written-communication

https://herbusiness.com/blog/effective-communication-begins-purpose/

What is effective written communication

https://grammar.yourdictionary.com/style-and-usage/what-is-effective-writing-communication.html

This is the most in demand skills on job listing right now

https://www.fastcompany.com/90556370/this-is-the-most-in-demand-skill-in-job-listings-right-now

The importance of written communication skills (SHRM)

https://www.shrm.org/resourcesandtools/hr-topics/organizational-and-employee-development/career-advice/pages/the-importance-of-written-communication-skills.aspx

Chapter 3.0

https://www.nature.com/scitable/topicpage/audience-and-purpose-13952663/#:~:text=When%20you%20communicate %2C%20your%20purpose,must%20adapt%20to%20your%20audience.

Chapter 4.0

https://courses.lumenlearning.com/suny-esc-communicationforprofessionals/chapter/purpose/

Chapter 5.0

https://www.youthfully.ca/narrative-communication-skills/

Chapter 6.0

https://medium.com/dc-design/what-is-human-centered-design-6711c09e2779

MECE Principle (Wikipedia)

https://en.wikipedia.org/wiki/MECE_principle

Barbara Minto: "MECE: I invented it, so I get to say how to pronounce it"

https://www.mckinsey.com/alumni/news-and-events/global-news/

alumni-news/barbara-minto-mece-i-invented-it-so-i-get-to-say-how-to-pronounce-it

MECE (Mutually Exclusive Collectively Exhaustive)

https://www.caseinterview.com/mece

MECE Framework McKinsey

https://www.mbacrystalball.com/blog/strategy/mece-framework/

MECE Principle: The Ultimate Guide to MECE Frameworks

https://hackingthecaseinterview.thinkific.com/pages/mece

Chapter 11

The power of the one page strategic plan

https://onstrategyhq.com/resources/the-power-of-the-one-page-strategic-plan/https://www.slideteam.net/blog/top-5-one-page-communication-plan-templates

https://www.slideteam.net/blog/top-10-one-page-communication-plan-for-formulating-effective-business-strategy

Sun Tzu – The Art of War

https://medium.com/@kwharrison13/the-art-of-war-book-review-quotes-d599462cd80b#:~:text=%E2%80%9CIf%20words%20of%20command%20are,the%20fault%20of%20their%20officers.%E2%80%9D

Notes

www.ingramcontent.com/pod-product-compliance
Lightning Source LLC
LaVergne TN
LVHW091512170726
843492LV00001B/460